Grégoire Solotareff

DON'T CALL ME LITTLE BUNNY

LONDON
VICTOR GOLLANCZ LTD
1988

There was once a rabbit whom everyone called Little Bunny. That wasn't his real name. His real name was Jack Carrot. Jack didn't understand why the grown-ups, who had normal names just like his own, called him Little Bunny.

Jack's grandfather explained, "Grown-ups call you Little Bunny because they think small rabbits are cute and cuddly. Later, when you're older, they will just call you Jack."

The time did come when all the grown-ups said, "My, haven't you grown!" But they still called him Little Bunny.

On top of that, Jack heard two rabbits his own age talking about him. "Look at Little Bunny," one of them said. "He looks a bit taller. His ears are longer, anyway!"

Jack was miserable. He didn't have a single friend. "Something must be done," he said to himself. "First, I am small. Right. Second, I am a rabbit. OK. To make people stop calling me Little Bunny, I am going to become the most rascally rabbit anyone has ever seen."

He started by making faces at the mama rabbits who patted his cheek and called him Little Bunny. When one of them gave him a sweet, he threw it down and stamped on it. Then he stole some carrots.

Things went from bad to worse.

Armed with a real pistol, a bow and arrows, a very pointy dagger and a sword, he held up a bank.

"Nobody move! Put your hands in the air! This is a hold-up!"

The bank manager gave him all the money in the safe, then called the police.

Jack had no use for the money. He only wanted to strike fear in the hearts of people and rabbits.

He heard the sirens and quickly made his escape.

"There he goes!" cried the police,
in hot pursuit.

There was a long chase in the forest, across a field,
then back into the woods. It was terrible.

A policeman lunged for his skis, and Jack fainted into a snow-drift.

When he awoke, he was in prison. The
police had taken his weapons and he was all
alone. It was dark. He began to cry.

"Hello," said a small rabbit. "You mustn't cry like that. I'm Jim Radish. Who are you?"

"Jack. Jack Carrot."

"What a funny name! Come on, have a biscuit and tell me how they caught you."

Jack told his story up to the moment he had fainted. Jim listened closely.

"Don't worry," he said. "We're getting out of here. I have a plan."

Jack jumped to his feet. Then he saw that Jim was even smaller than himself. He laughed and laughed — he couldn't help it. Jim, who was a good sport, laughed too.

Finally they stopped laughing, and Jack asked, "So what about you? Why did they put you in prison?"

"Because I killed a hunter," answered Jim.

"Killed a hunter! That's horrible!"

"It's not horrible. If I hadn't killed him, he would've killed me."

"Really?" said Jack. "But why?"

"To eat me, why do you think, Little Bunny?"

Jack had to laugh. A rabbit even smaller than he, calling him Little Bunny. It was too much.

"Listen!" he said. "If you call me Little Bunny, I will call you Sprout and bunnies *eat* sprouts, you know."

Jim shook his fist at him, but the two were only joking.

To escape the prison, Jack and Jim dug a tunnel. It was a speciality of theirs, after all.

As soon as they reached the outside, the two rabbits ran to the
forest as fast as they could.

Once out of danger, Jack and Jim vowed to stick together for ever.

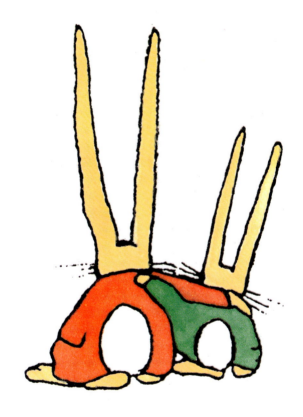

They decided to go to Jack's grandfather's house. They were cold
and hungry and they knew he would take care of them.

At last they reached Grandfather's home.
"Look how much bigger I am," Jack said.
Jim Radish laughed. He didn't mind being the smallest.

The old rabbit hid them in a secret burrow high in the mountains where the police never went. He brought them food and blankets, chocolate, chewing gum and the evening paper. Across the front page, the headline said:

GREAT ESCAPE OF TWO LITTLE BUNNIES

Jack and Jim found this vastly funny.

They have stayed in their mountain hide-out ever since. Jack's grandfather visits them often.

One day, when the police have forgotten about them, they will leave their hiding place. But they are in no hurry to go.

Originally published in France 1987
by l'école des loisirs
under the title *Ne M'appelez Plus Jamais ‹Mon Petit Lapin›*

First published in Great Britain 1988
by Victor Gollancz Ltd
14 Henrietta Street, London WC2E 8QJ

Illustrations © 1988 by l'école des loisirs, Paris
English text © 1988 by Farrar, Straus & Giroux, Inc.

Adapted from the translation by Naomi Lewis

British Library Cataloguing in Publication Data
Solotareff, Grégoire
Don't call me little bunny.
I. Title II. Ne m'appelez plus jamais
"mon petit lapin". *English*
843′.914[J]

ISBN 0-575-04252-4

Printed in Hong Kong by Imago Publishing Ltd